Our Planet Earth

Story by **Christian Grenier**
Factual accounts
and activities by **François Aulas**

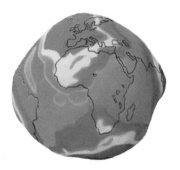

BARRON'S

contents

Story

Mega-infos

Activity

Mega-infos

Activity

Mega-infos

Game

Mega-infos

Quiz

Index

Answers

Anecdotes

Stickers

Mega-infos

Picture Cards

Prisoner of the Eocene

Christian Grenier

A Strange Machine

"Yes, Remy, this machine can travel through time!"

I thought Grandpa Luke was joking. In his laboratory, the only thing I saw was a gigantic egg whose top was touching the ceiling. He added: "What's annoying is that I'm too chubby to test it myself . . ."

Chubby? Let's just say that Grandpa Luke's enormous!

"But you, Remy, you're young, flexible, and wiry . . ."

"Me? Yes, Grandpa, but I'm not crazy!"

"Come on, you'll make a very brief leap into prehistory and

you'll bring back some photos and an animal. I thought about a lemur: the adapis."

"Gosh! Why not an apatosaurus or a diplodocus?"

"Because an adapis is the size of a squirrel. And they're also our ancestors, Remy! Imagine our success within the scientific world!"

What came over me? Well, I love my Grandpa Luke. I trust him; he's a great scientist. In fact, I was fascinated by the idea of traveling to the past. I said yes. So I climbed into the egg! Sitting in the only seat, I had three pedals at my feet and, facing me, a screen and a small steering wheel.

"You change speeds with this lever. If you turn the wheel to the left, you'll go back into the past; to return to the present, turn it to the right. Hmm . . . the gauge shows the date . . ." Grandpa Luke closed the door. Although we'd stay in contact by radio, I wasn't feeling very secure.

I brought along an encyclopedia to identify the plants and animals of the past. I started the engine, put it into first gear, and turned the wheel. Why, this machine wasn't any more difficult to drive than a car.

"You did it," Grandpa Luke's voice said to me. "The egg has disappeared! You're on your way, Remy!"

I could scarcely believe it. The screen was a kaleidoscope of colors. Numbers were flying by on the gauge. Once it

passed fifty million years ago, I stopped. I found myself in the middle of an incredible valley.

"Grandpa Luke? Can you hear me? I think I've made it!"

"Wonderful, Remy! Tell me what you see."

"Snow-capped peaks! Here . . . in the middle of the high plateaus? Impossible!"

"Why yes, Remy, quite possible. During the Eocene, the mountains were younger."

I opened the door. The air felt hot, humid, and fragrant. I recognized laurel and magnolias amid the thick grass. What a paradise!

Oh, I spoke too quickly: As I ventured into the jungle, all of a sudden I was facing some kind of giant ostrich with a lizard's head.

"Oh, no! . . . Run!"

The monster bolted when it saw me: it had been more scared than I! My encyclopedia informed me that it was a diatryma. The adapis sounded a lot nicer. But how could I lure one out? After an hour of futile searching, I was resigned to going back. Then I saw a small mammal prowling around my egg. There was no doubt, it was the legendary adapis!

Lost in the Past!

The animal didn't seem wild. He let me pet him, then lead him into the time machine.

"Grandpa Luke? I did it! I got what you wanted. I'm coming back . . ." Oh, that dratted animal! Before I could react, the adapis had pulled off the steering wheel and run back into the jungle with it. Panic-stricken, I ran after him: "Adapis! Come back! Come here right now!"

But no, the lemur didn't obey. He and I played hide-and-seek for hours. It was getting dark. Depressed, I returned to my egg.

"Grandpa Luke? It's a disaster. I've lost the adapis—and the steering wheel!"

"It's too bad about the animal, but you can return to the present without a steering wheel, Remy. A screwdriver will do the trick. Look under the seat; you'll find a tool box there."

It was incredible. Trapped in the Eocene, I had to use an ordinary screwdriver to escape! I tried to leave. The screen became blurred.

"Well?" Grandpa Luke asked. "Is it working?"

"I don't know, the time dial is blank."

"Stop in a quarter of an hour and go out, then you'll see!"

When I partly opened the door of the machine, I wasn't at all reassured. A squall of rain burst into the cockpit. I

called out: "Grandpa Luke? It's incredible—the egg is sinking into a swamp. I'm surrounded by gigantic forests. It's hot and . . . why, yes, I see the ocean in the distance!"

"Uh . . . Remy, you must have made a wrong turn. In my opinion, you've leapt 50 million years backwards and you are in the Mesozoic era!"

When I saw the enormous shape of a diplodocus, I knew that Grandpa Luke was correct. Poor me! What would happen to me if I kept going backwards like that? I'd end up reaching the Paleozoic era, or even the time when the Earth was a ball of flame. My egg would soon be cooked! So I got underway again, carefully turning the screwdriver to the right. After twenty minutes of flying blindly, I stopped the engine to take a quick glance outside. This time, an intense cold invaded the cockpit.

In the twilight, I saw some prehistoric men crouching around a fire at the mouth of a cave. I quickly took a picture and closed the door again. I explained to Grandpa Luke what I'd seen.

"Perfect!" he exclaimed. "You entered one of the ice ages of the Quaternary. You're getting closer to the present. Listen carefully, Remy. According to my calculations, you should make exactly—hmm—six and a half turns!"

Full of hope, I did so.

Story

A Leap into the Future

Opening the door, I found myself face-to-face with a multi-colored crowd that seemed to be waiting for me: so many different colors of skin, so many different faces! You'd have thought that most of the people of the Earth had gathered here! Suddenly, I saw Grandpa Luke coming toward me, accompanied by someone who looked a lot like him. But I know my grandfather is an only child! More and more astonished, I saw, not far from them, an egg that resembled my own.

"Welcome to the future, Remy," Grandpa Luke said to me.

"Would you allow us to retrieve the adapis?" his twin asked me.

I then discovered the animal. It had hidden, and fallen asleep, behind my seat! The two men handed me a wheel similar to the one I'd lost. They smiled at me with a strange kindliness.

"There. You'll rejoin your present. Go on! And who knows, Remy . . . see you soon?"

My surprise had left me speechless. As soon as I put the new steering wheel into place, the numbers appeared on the dials. I was in the year 2060! Daydreaming about it, I went back into the past. This time, I rejoined the present with no difficulty. When I reappeared in the laboratory, Grandpa

Luke threw himself into my arms. He seemed very moved, as was I.

"Remy! I was so afraid. You were right, it was a dangerous trip."

"Oh, Grandpa Luke, I don't have the adapis. I had to leave it in the . . . what an incredible story! Listen, I can tell you everything—but I didn't understand anything!" My trip to the year 2060 intrigued him greatly. Suddenly he exclaimed, "Remy, I understand. Going into the future, what a dream! To meet the representatives of all those nations gathered together . . ."

His face was alight with excitement and cunning, and I was more and more disturbed. The next day, I returned with the developed photos. But Grandpa Luke wasn't there. I checked the laboratory. The egg had disappeared! The only thing left was the seat, dismantled. Worried, I noticed a letter on the table.

Dear Remy,

I've left in my machine for the year 2059. I will not be coming back to the present. But one day we'll meet again . . . yes, think about it—but you'll have to be patient! When you meet me again, we'll wait for the egg from the past to appear. You'll come out—or rather, the child you were will come out, the very one you are today. Then, we'll retrieve the adapis from under your seat . . .

In a few minutes I'll meet you again, but grown old,
while you, Remy, still have many years to wait!

See you soon . . . or later—you decide.

Your old Grandpa Luke

I reread my grandfather's letter ten times. Now I under-
stood everything. In a good half-century, I would, at last,
see the egg in which Grandpa Luke had left reappear in this
laboratory. Wait, I'll have to wait . . .

It seems as though I've already grown some. But it's
impossible to rush the course of time. I feel like a prisoner,
trapped in this present which moves forward all too slowly
for my liking.

The year 2059! I am so impatient to be there and to see
Grandpa Luke again, so we can go on our explorations of
time together!

The Solar System

About 15 billion years ago, when nothing yet existed, there was a great explosion...

▨ And Then There Was Light...
The Big Bang❦ ! It's the beginning of the universe. The stars are born and gather into galaxies. Ten billion years later, a small nebula, a cloud of gas and dust, collapses on itself and gives birth to our solar system. The cloud flattens into the form of a disk. In the center, the Sun "catches fire."

> ❦ *Big Bang*
> *An expression for the great explosion in which our universe was born.*

Jupiter

The Sun

Earth

Mercury   Mars

Venus

Mega-infos

▌ The Law of Gravity

Like the Moon around the Earth, the planets revolve around the Sun, thanks to a force which acts over a distance: gravity. Bodies attract one another according to their mass and the distance that separates them. It was by watching some falling apples that Sir Isaac Newton, a physicist and astronomer, discovered the law of gravity.

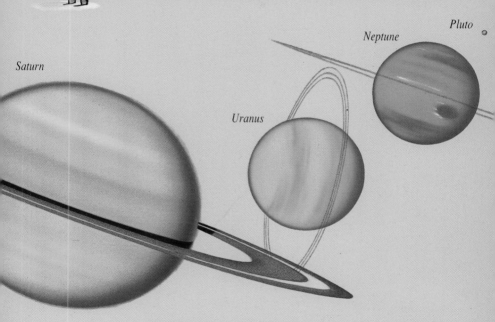

Saturn

Uranus

Neptune

Pluto

▌ Rocky or Gaseous Planets?

The dust of the nebula gathered and formed four rocky planets, those nearest the Sun: Mercury, Venus, Earth, and Mars. Farther away, the gases accumulated around four giant planets composed of rocks and gases: Jupiter, Saturn, Uranus, and Neptune. A ninth planet, Pluto, revolves at the edges of the solar system with other frozen rocks.

ur equipment, observe the shadow
the Sun upon the Earth, the phases
loon following its movement around
th, and the eclipses of the Moon.

1. Straighten the hanger and
make it into the shape of a bow.
At one end, make a loop the
size of the can. Make a second
loop, which will hold the support
for the Moon.

2. Bend the thin piece of
end around a pencil, mak
around the large supporti
second loop. That way, th
will turn freely around the

the Earth and the Moon

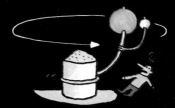

3. Pierce the two balls completely through. Paint the tennis ball blue to make it look like Earth. The Ping-Pong ball (the Moon) stays white. Place the two balls on their supports. Bend the wire under the Earth to lock it into place.

4. Fill the can with sand. Place it inside the large loop. Make sure that the two balls are turning on a horizontal plane (it's called an elliptical plane), parallel to the table on which the can is sitting.

5. Stick the candle in the sand. Ask an adult to light it: It's the Sun! Make it dark inside the room.

The Beginnings of Life

For a long time, the Earth remained lifeless. Billions of years passed before life appeared and took hold on our planet.

■ Volcanic Jolts

A terrible heat dominates the first ages of the Earth. Numerous volcanoes spit out gases, steam, and lava. Thick clouds abound in an atmosphere of burning carbon gas. It's very hot, a bit like Venus nowadays.

■ Torrential Rains

Then the volcanoes become a little more peaceful. The Earth cools and solidifies. With an atmosphere full of water vapor, it begins to rain. It rains for millions of years, enough to fill the oceans with 322,300,000 cubic miles (1347 million cubic km) of water. What a downpour! The continents and oceans form, but the atmosphere is still poisonous and life cannot yet appear in the open air. This situation continues for another billion years.

And Then There Was Life...

Blue algae appears in the oceans around 3.8 billion years ago. They colonize it for 3 billion years. Old traces of them can be found in ancient rocks in Greenland. **Photosynthesis** begins 2.8 billion years ago. Little by little, the atmospheric proportion of oxygen increases to the present-day figure of 21%. Finally, 570 million years ago, organisms with body parts that were preserved as fossils became more numerous.

❦ Photosynthesis
Green plants absorb carbon dioxide for nourishment and make oxygen as a byproduct.

Evolution

300 million years ago, earliest reptiles appear.

Continuous Change: Plants and animals diversify through the process of evolution.

■ **A Succession of Ice Ages**

Over the last two million years, the Earth has undergone around fifty ice ages. The glaciers covered a third of the globe, all the way to the latitude of New York or Lyons, France, then they melted. The last Ice Age came to a close ten thousand years ago. **Flora**❣ and **fauna**❣ adapt to meet each of these climatic changes.

248 million years

144 million years

65 million years

❣ *Fauna and Flora*
Fauna means all of the animal species and flora, all of the plant species.

The dinosaurs dominated the Earth for about 165 million years. Then they disappeared suddenly, along with other species, after the impact of a meteor 65 million years ago. Crashing into the ground, the meteor threw dust into the atmosphere, which darkened the sky.

Mega-infos

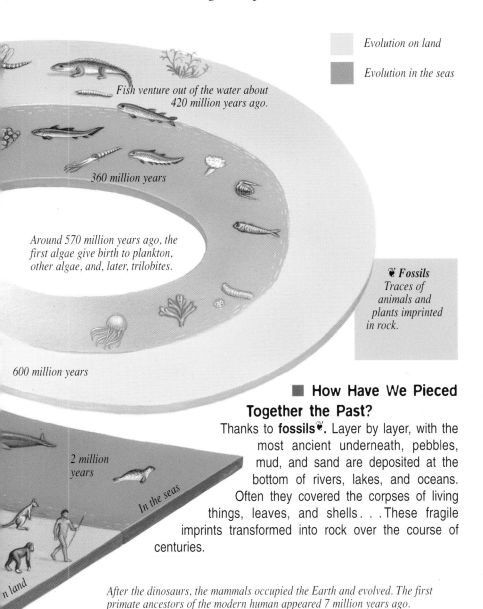

Evolution on land

Evolution in the seas

Fish venture out of the water about 420 million years ago.

360 million years

Around 570 million years ago, the first algae give birth to plankton, other algae, and, later, trilobites.

❧ Fossils
Traces of animals and plants imprinted in rock.

600 million years

2 million years

In the seas

n land

■ How Have We Pieced Together the Past?

Thanks to **fossils❧**. Layer by layer, with the most ancient underneath, pebbles, mud, and sand are deposited at the bottom of rivers, lakes, and oceans. Often they covered the corpses of living things, leaves, and shells. . .These fragile imprints transformed into rock over the course of centuries.

After the dinosaurs, the mammals occupied the Earth and evolved. The first primate ancestors of the modern human appeared 7 million years ago.

The Earth and

Thought to have formed after the Earth, the Moon ceaselessly revolves around it.

The Earth

age: 4.65 billion years

diameter at the Equator: 7,926 miles (12,756 km)

diameter at the Poles: 7,899.83 miles (12,714 km)

mass: 6.6 sextillion short tons (6.0 sextillion metric tons)

average distance from the Sun: 92,900,000 miles (149,500,000 km). It is the third planet from the Sun and lies between Venus and Mars.

length of a revolution around the Sun: 365.26 days

the incline of the orbit compared to the Equator: 23°27′

the speed traveling around the Sun: 66,600 mph (107,200 km/h)

average temperature of the surface: 57° F (14 °C)

internal temperature: between 1,600 and 13,000° F (870 and 7,000 °C)

thickness of the atmosphere: 99% is less than 50 miles (80 km)

Its Satellite

The Moon

age: 4.0 billion years

diameter: 2,160 miles (3,476 km)

mass: 80.9 trillion tons (73.5 trillion metric tons), that is, 81 times less than the Earth

average distance from the Earth: 238,857 miles (384,402 km)

length of a revolution around the Earth: 27.32 days

◼ Geographical References

To get one's bearing on the Earth, an imaginary grid has been devised made up of parallels, which indicate latitude, and meridians, which indicate longitude.

the Tropic of Cancer   *a meridian*   *the geographic North Pole*

the Equator

the Tropic of Capricorn

a parallel   *the South Pole*

The Interior of the Ear

Protected by a thin crust below our feet, the planet is very hot. It is formed of rocks and metal.

A Hot Planet

When the Earth is mined, the temperature rises around 1° F (.56 °C) for every 100 feet (30 m) of depth. The deepest of these mines is in Zapl'amy in Russia, which goes down 7.2 miles (12 km). The temperature there exceeds 572° F (300 °C). Below 42 miles (70 km) in depth, it is more than 1,832° F (1,000 °C). Luckily, the Earth's crust protects us from this infernal, internal heat.

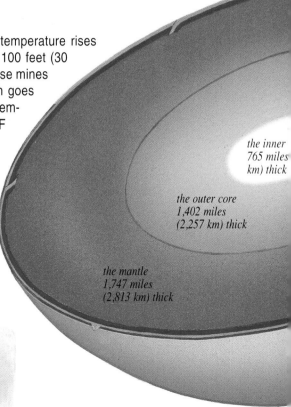

*the inner
765 miles
km) thick*

*the outer core
1,402 miles
(2,257 km) thick*

*the mantle
1,747 miles
(2,813 km) thick*

Mega-infos

■ The Earth's Crust

The surface of the Earth, called the lithosphere, is cold and hard. It is a shell of stone 43.5 miles (70 km) thick beneath the mountains and 5 miles (8 km) thick below the oceans. This layer, which is relatively light, floats like a raft on the mantle. It has fractured into a dozen plates, pieces of the crust which drift in relationship to each other.

the litho-sphere, 4.8 to 42 miles (8–70 km) thick

■ The Mantle

The mantle consists of three layers: two of solid rock sandwiching one of semiliquid material. The temperature ranges from about 2,372° F (1,300 °C) at the top to about 9,302° F (5,000 °C) at the bottom. It is 1,747 miles (2,813 km) thick. Immense convection currents agitate the thick **magma**.

☙ Magma
Hot, melted rocks

■ The Outer Core

Between 1,402 and 3,180 miles (2,257–5,150 km) deep, the outer core is composed of liquid iron and nickel, at 9,032° F (5,000 °C). Inside the outer core is the solid inner core, which is 765 miles (1,231 km) thick.

PTiou

The Earth Is a Magnet

The Earth is a giant magnet that cloaks us in a protective magnetic field. It is still the source of many mysteries.

The invisible "lines of force" indicate the direction and orientation of the magnetic field.

■ A Protective Force

The magnetic field is beneficial. It repels back into space dangerous particles called "solar winds" produced by the Sun. It thus protects life on the surface of the Earth. The active zone of the Earth's magnetic field is called the magnetosphere and stretches far into space.

■ The Earth, a Great Magnet

To find your way on land or sea, a compass is a sure thing. The planet is a great magnet which always directs the compass needle in the same direction: North-South. But where does this force come from?

By turning along with the Earth's rotation, the metallic core making up the center of the Earth produces a magnetic field, like an electric generator.

The geographic North Pole

The magnetic North P

A Gorgeous Spectacle

The Sun sometimes throws off enormous bursts of particles that travel to the Earth and produce magnetic storms. These are solar eruptions. When this happens, the solar wind becomes violent and the magnetic field is less effective in protecting the Earth. Electrified particles, electrons, penetrate the atmosphere around 187 miles (300 km) deep and produce light shows in the sky such as the *aurora borealis* (the Northern Lights).

The aurora borealis is only visible in polar regions.

The North Pole on a Stroll

If, for us, the magnetic North Pole almost coincides with the geographical North Pole, it hasn't always been the case. In the course of its long history, the Earth has often lost the north! Many times, the North Pole has moved and has even flip-flopped from the North to the South. Why? It's a mystery. That's a good reason for getting lost!

Well now!

According to my compass...

...I'm at the North Pole!

How Not to Lose the

Is the Earth really a magnet? To prove it, all you need to do is let a small, movable compass point spontaneously...

Make a Compass

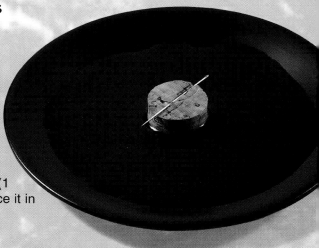

1. Cut a half-inch-thick (1 cm) disk off a cork. Place it in water.

2. Magnetize the needle by rubbing it against a magnet in *one direction only* (do not go back and forth).

You need:
- a cork
- a knife
- a bowl full of water
- a needle
- a magnet

3. Lay the needle on the cork. It will point toward the North: It's a compass.

(Magnetic!) North Pole

The True Direction of the North

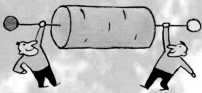

1. Poke a pin into each end of a cork and place the cork on a glass. It should turn freely.

You need:
• a cork
• a glass
• a needle
• two pins
• a magnet

2. Magnetize the needle by rubbing it on a magnet (in one direction only), then pierce the cork all the way through the center.

3. Place the cork on the glass, pointing the needle toward the North. The needle will tilt to get its direction with respect to the lines of force of the Earth's magnetic field.

The Protective Layer

All kinds of dangerous rays come here from the sun. Luckily, the atmosphere protects us.

◼ A Meteor Trap

The gases of the atmosphere protect the planet from the fall of small meteors, which burn upon contacting the dense air. Shooting stars are the bright traces of this.

◼ Ozone, an Efficient Filter

Between 12 and 30 miles (19–49 km) in altitude, a layer of **ozone** covers the Earth as a protective cover. It absorbs ultraviolet rays, a form of solar rays that are very harmful to all living things. They can cause serious sunburns and cancer. Ozone thereby protects life.

❦ Ozone
A particularly toxic form of elemental oxygen.

◼ The Greenhouse Effect: Unheard-of Luck

The solar rays pass through the atmosphere (1) and heat the ground (2). The Earth sheds the heat into space (3). The atmosphere traps this heat. This is the Greenhouse Effect (4). With it, it's neither too hot nor too cold. Without this effect, the average temperature on Earth would be just below 0° F (–18 °C), rather than the current 57° F (14 °C) median.

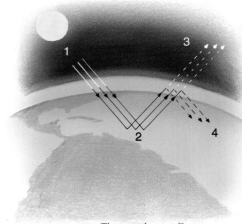

The greenhouse effect

■ The Protective Layers of Air

The atmosphere is a gaseous envelope about 600 miles (1,000 km) thick composed of oxygen (21%), nitrogen (78%), argon and other rare gases (1%), and water vapor.

The thermosphere lies between 50 and 300 miles (80–480 km) above the Earth's surface. The temperature there can exceed 1,800° F (1,000 °C). The exosphere of thin gases begins beyond it.

Above 30 miles (50 km) in altitude, in the mesosphere where it drops as low as –130° F (–90 °C), the air grows thin.

Between 8 and 30 miles (12.9–50 km) lies the dry stratosphere. It contains ozone.

Near the ground, in the tropo-sphere (between 0 and 10 miles, or 0–16 km), clouds make for rain or a sunny day.

Continental

The Earth's crust is always moving. Slowly but surely, the continents are drifting.

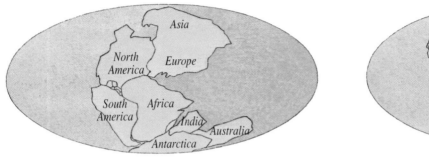

1. About 200 million years ago, the continental mass, which before was made up of only a single piece, began to break into fragments.

■ The Moving Walkway

The surface of the Earth seems to stand still. However, it's moving! The continents are solid plates which float on thick magma. Pushed by the movements of the mantle, a dozen plates slowly drift, as though on a moving walkway. They're called tectonic plates.

■ Wegener, a Visionary

A German meteorologist, Alfred Wegener, had an insight about continental drift. He noticed that the coasts of South America and Africa could fit into one another. Moreover, certain fossils found on the two continents were identical, as though in prehistoric times there was a single landmass, which is now divided in two.

Drift

2. *Each slab is drifting in a different direction. India, for instance, has embedded itself in Asia.*

3. *Nowadays, the plates continue to drift. Africa is slowly getting closer to Europe, and in 20 million years the Mediterranean Sea will disappear.*

■ The Movements of the Earth

Along the **oceanic ridges**🐾 each year, two plates get farther and farther apart at the rate of .4 to 4.5 inches (1–12 cm) a year. On the other hand, when two plates collide, the heavier one thrusts under the lighter one in a process called subduction. Along the zones of contact, there are areas rubbing together which are responsible for earthquakes and the appearance of volcanoes.

> 🐾 *Oceanic Ridges*
> *Mountain chains lying under water, in the mid-Atlantic for example.*

1. The Earth's crust is breaking in northern Africa. It will create a new ocean several million years from now.

2. The mid-Atlantic ridge.

Volcanic Smoke

Volcanoes, which are directly linked to magma, attest to the forces that agitate the Earth's mantle.

▪ Stacked Plates

When two plates of the Earth's crust meet one another, the friction of the rocks gives birth to a volcanic zone. More than 475 volcanoes, out of about 1,500 active ones, are on the edges of the plates. They are located around the Pacific Ocean (the Ring of Fire), in Indonesia, and in the Mediterranean.

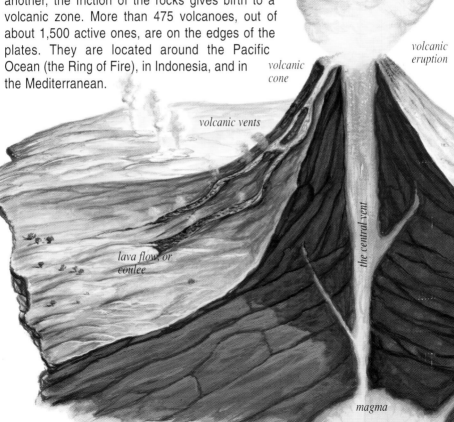

volcanic eruption

volcanic cone

volcanic vents

the central vent

lava flow, or coulee

magma

ash and smoke

■ Hot Spots

In certain places, a "hot spot" pierces the Earth's crust for unknown reasons. It can cause the birth of a volcano, which can become extinct or spread widely. This is how the Hawaiian Islands were formed, and also the volcanoes of Hoggar in Africa.

■ Show Me How Your Lava Flows...

...and I'll tell you what you are. Volcanic eruptions are classified according to the manner in which their lava flows, often named after well-known volcanoes with similar behavior.

■ The Volcanic Cone

A volcano is composed of a central vent connecting it with the liquid lava of the deep magma. Ashes and lava form a mountain with a crater at the summit. Observing a volcano, measuring its growth, its tremors, and its ventings, sometimes allows scientists to predict eruptions and evacuate residents in time. Be careful, any sleeping volcano could reawaken one day!

The Pelean type:
The lava is very viscous and has burning clouds.

The Vulcanian type:
The lava is viscous with clouds of ashes.

The Strombolian type:
The lava is not very thick.

The Hawaiian type:
The lava is very fluid and flows rapidly.

The Life and Death

Enormous and domineering, mountains, born from the movement of the planet, always end up disappearing.

The Formation of Mountains

The appearance of mountains is the result of extremely violent collisions between continents. When two plates meet, one blocks the other. Under the shock, the rocks begin folding, shortening, and thickening. This is how mountains are formed.

Some record heights

Mont Blanc (France) 15,771 feet (4,807 m)	Kenya (Kenya) 17,058 feet (5,199 m)	Kilimanjaro (Tanzania) 19,340 feet (5,875 m)	McKinley (United States) 20,320 feet (6,194 m)	Aconcagua (Argentina) 22,834 feet (6,960 m)	K-2 (Godwin-Austen) (Kashmir) 28,250 feet (8,611 m)	Everest (Nepal-Tibet) 29,028 feet (8,848 m)

# of Mountains

Worn Summits

The slope causes rocks to tumble down, water to flow, glaciers to slide. Little by little, the rain, the ice, and the wind wear down the rocks. That's erosion. The ice smoothes the bottoms of valleys. Over several million years, mountains become plains.

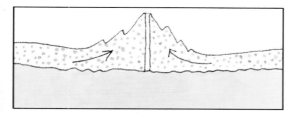

The formation of the Himalayas: The Indian plate collides with that of Asia, which folds.

Young or Old

Young mountains like the Andes, the Alps, or the Himalayas have been rising very slightly every year for more than 60 million years. On the other hand, the more aged mountains, which are 300 million years old, are no longer rising. They are being ground down by the effects of erosion.

Earthquakes

The collision of two plates causes blockage and slippage. From time to time, the earth quakes. More than a million seismic tremors are recorded every year. Despite numerous studies, earthquakes are still unpredictable.

Hurrah for Winter Sports! What a hubbu
on, 21 bizarre things have slipped into this sce

t this small ski resort! With so much going
an you find them? *Solution on page 63.*

The Immense Seas

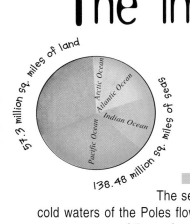

57.3 million sq. miles of land

Arctic Ocean
Atlantic Ocean
Indian Ocean
Pacific Ocean

138.48 million sq. miles of seas

Churned by currents, the oceans of the world represent about 70% of the surface of the Earth. They shape the coasts and soothe the extremes of the climate. They are still little explored.

■ Beneficial Currents

The seas are in a state of perpetual motion. The cold waters of the Poles flow like giant, submarine rivers beneath the warmer waters of the surface. Driven by winds, great currents cross the oceans. Thus, the Gulf Stream, which ranges from 50 miles (80 km) wide off the coast of Florida to 300 miles (480 km) wide off the coast of New York, crosses the Atlantic at an average speed of almost 3 mph (5 km/h), and warms the coast of Europe.

■ The Tides

The Moon attracts or repels the continents and seas. Every twelve hours, the continents rise (a maximum of 12 inches or 30 cm) because of the moon's attraction. This phenomenon is a land tide. For the waters of the seas and oceans, the motion is even more dramatic. In the Bay of Fundy in Nova Scotia, for example, the water can rise as much as 70 feet (21 m).

Chasms and mountains at the bottom of the oceans are mirrored on the surface.

■ The Ocean Has Bumps

People say the ocean is flat. Wrong! It sinks and has bumps everywhere. That's what observation satellites like the Topex-Poseidon and agencies such as NOAA have shown. The great currents and underwater topography deform the surface of the water. Now it is possible to measure the difference of levels of several yards within an inch or so (or several meters within a few centimeters).

The Earth as seen by satellite. The bumps are exaggerated.

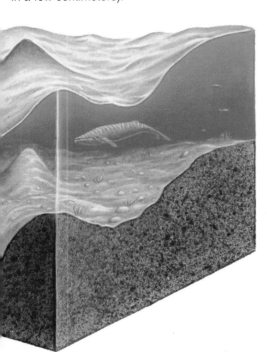

■ Why Is the Sea Salty?

Ever since the seas were formed, water has been running over rocks and dissolving them little by little. The minerals are deposited in the sea. Salt, the most soluble mineral, remains trapped in the water. Each quart of seawater contains about 1.24 ounces (35 g/L) of salt, or four teaspoons for every quart of water. There would be two truck-loads of 38.5 tons (35 metric tons) of salt in an Olympic-size pool full of seawater.

Water, a Necessity

From space, the planet Earth looks blue. That's the color of water, a gaseous, liquid, or solid element necessary for life.

The transportation of droplets in clouds

Precipitation in the form of rain or snow

Sea evaporation

Evaporation and transpiration from plants

well

fountain

■ The Power of Water

The flow of water hollows out deep valleys (the Grand Canyon, the Great Central Valley in California) and carries **alluvia❦**, which fill in deltas (the Mississippi, the Rhone, the Nile, or the Ganges). The water also dissolves limestone and digs out chasms and caves. Glaciers smooth valleys into a U-shape.

❦ *Alluvium*
Sand, gravel, and pebbles deposited on the bottom of flowing water.

■ Salt Water

The salty water of the oceans counts for 97.2% of the planet's water. By comparison, available fresh water in the atmosphere, above or below ground, only counts for .65% of global water. Glaciers trap 2.15% of the remaining water.

■ From the Sea and Back

Because of the effects of the Sun, water evaporates from the oceans, wet ground, and plants. While rising, the humid air cools. The water vapor condenses into tiny droplets and forms a cloud. The droplets join together to form rain, snow, or hail, depending on the temperature. The water falls back to the ground, then returns to the sea or evaporates on the spot. This is the great cycle of water.

The Cycle of Water
The salt water of the sea is transformed into fresh water (precipitation).

41

Climates

The Sun is the driving force of climates. The turbulent masses of air are moderated by the oceans.

■ The Sun: The Driving Force of Climates

The axis of the Earth's rotation inclines at 23°27′ in relationship to a vertical axis. For six months, one hemisphere is more exposed to the sun than the other, so the amount of sunshine and the length of the day change. Thus, the winter and summer are different, except at the Equator, where the amount of sun stays the same.

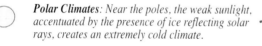

Polar Climates: Near the poles, the weak sunlight, accentuated by the presence of ice reflecting solar rays, creates an extremely cold climate.

Temperate Climates

 Continental: In the interior of continents, winters are harsh and summers hot.

 Oceanic: Influenced by the oceans, the air is filled with moisture. The climate is mild and humid.

 Mediterranean: Summers are dry and winters mild.

Between the Tropics

 Equatorial: Always getting the same amount of sunshine, the Equator has a warm climate with regular rain year-round.

 Tropical: On either side of the Equator, a dry season alternates with a wet one.

 Arid: The hot and cold deserts hardly ever receive any rain.

Mega-infos

■ Atmospheric Circulation

The atmosphere is crisscrossed with currents of air. When the air grows colder, it descends and exerts pressure, forming an area of high pressure. When it warms again, it becomes lighter, rises, and creates a depression. The winds from the high pressure areas flow toward the low-pressure areas. The warm air of the Equator rises toward the Poles, and that of the Poles, which is colder, descends toward the Equator.

The Climatic Zones of the World

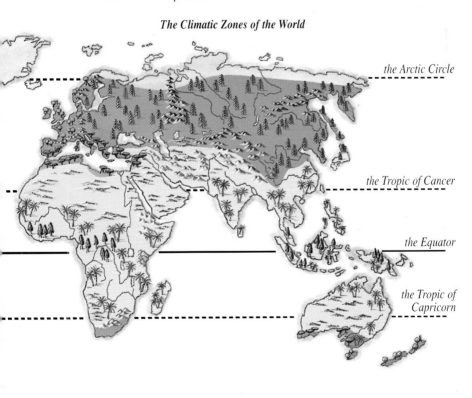

the Arctic Circle

the Tropic of Cancer

the Equator

the Tropic of Capricorn

the Antarctic Circle

What's the Weather

Clouds indicate what the weather is like or what it will be like. Observing them allows us to forecast wind gusts, storms, tornadoes, and hurricanes.

■ Clouds Indicate the Weather

Cirrus clouds indicate passing storms.

Cumulonimbus clouds indicate thunderstorms, hail, and, rarely, tornadoes.

Altocumulus clouds may signify bad weather.

Cumulus clouds are a sign of good weather in the summer.

Like?

■ Thunderstorms

Thunderstorms are caused by the rise and rapid cooling of hot air inside a cumulonimbus cloud. The appearance of electric charges produces lightning and thunder before abundant precipitation of rain or snow.

■ Floods

When it rains too long or too hard or also during the snow-melt, rivers overflow and cause sometimes-catastrophic floods. Human development can increase the damage by blocking drainage or the flow of water.

Cirrocumulus clouds indicate a worsening of the weather.

Stratocumulus clouds cause very light showers.

■ Monsoons

The rains of the monsoons watering Asia every year are caused by humid masses of oceanic air. They are driven by the air located over the Himalayas, which re-heats more rapidly. During the two months of the annual monsoons, almost 34 feet (10 m) of rain might fall.

Incredibl

HIGH

RECORDS

The tallest point on the surface of the Earth is Mt. Everest, which reaches 29,028 feet (8,848 m) above sea level. The Mariana Trench, southwest of Guam, descends to 36,198 feet (11,033 m) below the surface of the sea. It is the Earth's deepest point.

LOW

VARIABLE WEATHER

In the mountains, the weather can change very rapidly. Sometimes these variations are truly amazing: In 1943, in South Dakota, the temperature went from −4° F to 44.6° F (−20 °C to +7 °C) . . . in 2 minutes. In 1916, in Montana, it jumped 99 F° (55 C°) between the day (44° F or 6.7 °C) and night (−55.8° F or −48.8 °C).

but True!

● IT'S GROWING!

The SPOT satellite allows us to photograph the surface of the Earth from space. Every 22 days, the satellite passes over the same spot. It is possible, therefore, to monitor the rate of plant growth in a field or problems in a forest. We can finally observe the health of the planet live!

■ A SERIES OF CATASTROPHES

Volcanoes are killer mountains. On the island of Martinique in 1902, Mt. Pelée exploded and, in two minutes, killed all but one of the estimated 30,000 inhabitants of the town of Saint-Pierre. Catastrophes every bit as enormous can still take place because volcanoes are so unpredictable.

Life Everywhere

All over the Earth, a fragile, rich, and varied life has developed. It has inhabited every area.

▨ Rich and Varied Environments

The Earth has been explored for thousands of years. Nonetheless, new plants, animals, and insects continue to be discovered, especially in the rain forests.

Animals in their natural setting

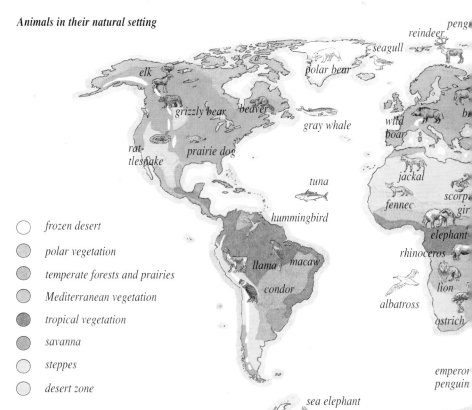

reindeer peng

seagull

polar bear

elk

grizzly bear beaver

gray whale

wild boar b

rat-tlesnake prairie dog

jackal

tuna

scorp

fennec gir

hummingbird

elephant

rhinoceros

llama macaw

condor

lion

albatross

ostrich

- ○ *frozen desert*
- ◔ *polar vegetation*
- ◑ *temperate forests and prairies*
- ◐ *Mediterranean vegetation*
- ● *tropical vegetation*
- ◕ *savanna*
- ○ *steppes*
- ○ *desert zone*

emperor penguin

sea elephant

Mega-infos

■ Around Hot Springs

Only ten years ago, it was thought that the bottom of the ocean was lifeless because of the lack of light. However, unknown species of worms, crabs, and octopuses have been discovered around hot springs of water bubbling from the ocean floor. In the complete darkness, they live on **bacteria**.

> **❦ Bacteria**
> *Microscopic creatures.*

■ In Cold or Heat

Every species has adapted to its environment. Mosses and lichens can grow on ice. Animals in cold regions are protected by thick fur and a thick layer of fat. The dry deserts are home to cactuses, scorpions...

An animal of the desert, the jerboa never drinks anything.

squirrel

wolf

bear

cormorant

omedary camel panda

tiger python

elephant

shark

kangaroo koala

blue whale

The toucan lives in the rain forests of South America.

The polar bear can tolerate temperatures down to −58° F (−50 °C).

All the Peoples of the Earth

Despite their numerous differences, all human beings resemble one another like members of the same family.

■ There Are No Races

We have been the descendants of *Homo sapiens* for 90,000 years. Petty differences (hair or skin color, height, the shape of the eyes or nose) are minor in comparison with our biological similarities (blood types...).

> **❦ Demography**
> *The science of the number of births and deaths, and the age of the population, of a country...*

STOP!

A street in India

■ A Demographic Stampede

Since the beginning of our species, a total of 8 billion human beings have been born, of which 6 billion are alive at present. This is a **demographic**❦ explosion. It will be necessary to control world population growth if it is to be limited to around 12 billion inhabitants in 100 years.

■ Density

The Earth's population is distributed unevenly. Certain countries have many inhabitants in a small area because the climate in those places is moderate and the land is fertile. Such is the case in the Netherlands (971 inhabitants per sq. mi.). Other countries are much more sparsely populated (Australia: 6 per sq. mi.) because of the aridity of the land or the harshness of the climate. Asia, with 3.4 billion inhabitants, is the most densely populated continent. South America is the least densely peopled.

■ Urban and Poor Above All

Currently, more than three-quarters of the world's population lives in cities. Two of the world's largest cities, Mexico City (17 million inhabitants) and São Paulo (16.7 million inhabitants), are located in poor countries. They attract poor people from rural areas who are looking for work. Unemployment creates misery in shanty towns on the edges of the great cities. The lack of proper hygiene and pollution worsen living conditions.

The Impact of Human

The six billion inhabitants of the Earth farm, clear the lands, and pollute the water, the air, and the soil of the planet.

■ A Dirty Planet

There is only one Earth; it cannot regenerate itself. Nonetheless, human beings pollute its atmosphere, rivers, and seas with industrial waste. Toxic and hazardous waste products are stored, untreated. Already more than 2 billion Earthlings are breathing polluted air, while the forests suffer from acid rain.

Exhaust fumes, factories, acid rain, trash dumps, and pesticides are threatening the balance of our planet.

■ A Worrisome Assault

Humanity exploits the soil, the subterranean areas, the forests, and the layers of underground water without thinking of the consequences. Already, the Aral Sea is changing into a desert, Lake Baikal (the greatest reservoir of fresh water in the world) is polluted, and the Mediterranean Sea is dirty. Accidents become ecological disasters: oil spills, radiation leaks, toxic gas emissions...Only Antarctica has escaped industrialization for the present.

Activity

Conquering the World

In 150 years, the world's population has grown from one billion to six billion people who have to eat, dress, get about, and house themselves. The excessive consumption of natural resources (water, oil, wood, minerals, and so forth) has profoundly altered the balance of the planet.

The Planet in Danger

Now we know the dangers that threaten the planet. Unfortunately, the list is rather long.

■ A Hole Is Forming

In 1985, observation satellites noticed a hole in the ozone layer. This hole is caused by the increase of chlorine waste coming from industry. In a chemical reaction with the chlorine gas, the ozone decomposes and no longer performs its protective role. It is necessary, therefore, to limit the harmful emissions because chlorine remains in the stratosphere for decades.

■ Intensive Agriculture

In order to produce cereal grains and to nourish all the inhabitants of the globe, farmers use many chemical products. Fertilizers pollute the water, while insecticides are increasingly less effective. Now we are developing **genetically-engineered** plants without knowing the consequences for the environment.

❦ Genetic Engineering occurs when a characteristic of a plant is altered. The plant can thus resist insecticides, and can mature more quickly...

■ The Greenhouse Effect, a System Out of Order

For about a century, the **fossil fuels** used in industry, heating, and transportation have increased carbon dioxide and methane gaseous waste in the atmosphere. They amplify the greenhouse effect. The Earth is in danger of becoming too hot. If this happens, the level of the sea could rise and climates would be thrown out of balance.

❦ *Fossil Fuels*
Nonrenewable resources found in the ground (oil, coal, and natural gas).

■ Deforestation

In South America, 15% of the Amazon forest has been destroyed in order to be replaced with farmland, and the destruction continues. The consequences of deforestation are terrible: the soil erodes, the terrain washes away. Land that was once fertile becomes a desert. Numerous animal and plant species disappear. At present, a third of the planet is threatened by this phenomenon.

Our Fate Depends

Viewed from space, the Earth is tiny and surrounded by an infinite void. What other solution do we have but to safeguard our planet?

■ How Can the Earth Be Saved?

The planet must be maintained like an immense garden, with its farming areas, its pleasure areas, its wild spaces. The developed countries already are using "clean" technologies that no longer produce waste and that make recyclable products. But for poor countries, these solutions are too expensive. Helping one another is the only solution.

The bottles are gather in a large container.

A family buys gl bottles.

■ What Is Ecology?

The Earth possesses millions of living species, varied **ecosystems❦**, an atmosphere...To act upon the planet, it's necessary first of all to study the relationships between living creatures, from minuscule bacteria to human populations, and their environments. That is the role of ecology.

> ❦ **Ecosystem**
> A place (the sea, a desert, a forest) and all of the creatures that inhabit it.

Solely on Us

ecycling Glass

In a recycling factory, the bottles are crushed and the glass is melted.

Maintaining the Planet

To be effective, technology will have to serve the environment; it will need to use renewable resources (sun, wind) and **biodegradable** 💚 materials. It will also be necessary for us to care for the soil and forests and, above all, to control the growth of world population.

New bottles are made from the original material.

💚 **Biodegradable**
A biodegradable product decomposes and disappears, consumed by bacteria, mushrooms, algae...

Is World Government Necessary?

The world population must become conscious of the variety and fragility of the planet, for we are all concerned, whether we live in Brasilia, in Sydney, or in the Kalahari. A worldwide understanding would, no doubt, soon bring the rights and responsibilities of every individual into harmony.

The Earth is cooling slowly.

True. The Earth's core is slowly losing its energy.

The air above the Earth stands still.

False. The atmosphere is covered with currents of air, the wind.

Water can cut through rocks.

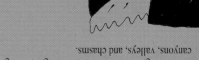

True. Along with the weather, flowing water digs canyons, valleys, and chasms.

Water was necessary for the appearance of life.

True. Life, without a doubt, began in the oceans. The water of our cells has almost the same composition as seawater.

False ?

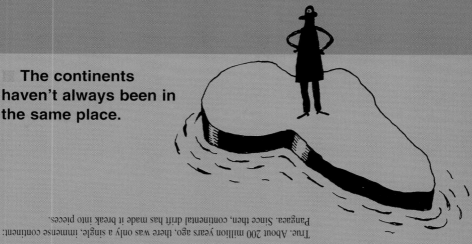

The continents haven't always been in the same place.

True. About 200 million years ago, there was only a single, immense continent: Pangaea. Since then, continental drift has made it break into pieces.

The rise in the greenhouse effect warms the climate.

True. By their activity (automobile traffic, agriculture, and industry), human beings produce waste gases which warm the atmosphere.

The Sun will die one day.

CLICK

True. It will go out in about 5 billion years. We still have time to get a tan!

Ozone is always beneficial.

OZONE PILLS

False. Ozone is a very toxic product for animals and plants. It is also used to disinfect pool water.

Quiz

CARAMBA

Mexico City will soon have more inhabitants than Australia.

True. It's the second largest city in the world and growing rapidly. Currently, 17 million people live here, while 18.6 million live in Australia.

The Earth is round.

False. The Earth isn't quite round. It is flattened at the Poles, and swollen at the Equator.

Mount Everest is the highest mountain on Earth.

False. An underwater volcano of 33,000 feet (10,000 m) in the Hawaiian Islands called Kilauea holds the record. Mount Everest is only 29,028 feet (8,848 m) tall.

The Sun is ten times bigger than the Earth.

False. It's a hundred times larger than the Earth.

False ?

Under our feet, the Earth is immobile and stable.

False. Land tides raise the continents almost a foot (30 cm) every 12 hours. "Small" earthquakes occur very frequently and continental drift is distancing Europe from America.

The climate of the Earth is getting warmer because of humankind.

Maybe. Nobody knows if the Earth gets warmer naturally or because of gaseous waste, which increases the greenhouse effect.

Extinct volcanoes are no longer dangerous.

False. Vesuvius, in Italy, was dormant for 1,000 years when it swallowed the city of Pompeii in the year 79 CE.

Antarctica is covered by a sheet of ice a half-mile (1 km) thick.

False. The ice sheet is 1.2 miles (2 km) thick.

Index

Answers to the puzzle on pages 36–37

You should have found: a pole missing on the ski lift, skiing trees, a skier leaving tire tracks, another skier going backwards, a water-skier, a man being pulled by a bird, a man in armor, a tennis ball amidst some snowballs, a bicyclist in the skating rink, flippers, a parrot, a man skiing backwards, a skiing snowman, a gorilla on a sled, a fakir with "magic carpet" skis, a man with a fan on his back, a skier using canes for poles, a decorated tree, a skier with a shovel, another skier with a baseball bat, a camel. There may be even more!

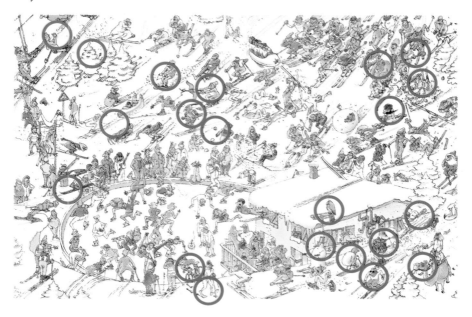

Activity Photographs
Edouard Chauvin

©1998 by Editions Nathan, Paris, France
The title of the French edition is *La Terre, notre planète.*
Published by Les Editions Nathan, Paris.

English translation © Copyright 1999 by Barron's Educational Series, Inc.

All inquiries should be addressed to:
Barron's Educational Series, Inc.
250 Wireless Boulevard
Hauppauge, New York 11788
http://www.barronseduc.com

Library of Congress Catalog Card No.: 98-74448
International Standard Book No.: 0-7641-5181-9

Printed in Italy
9 8 7 6 5 4 3 2 1

Stickers

A saguaro cactus in the Arizona desert

Symbols for sorting
out recyclables

Dinosaurs who lived from
195 to 65 million years ago

From 1417,
an ornate letter
P depicting
the Earth

A depiction
of the Earth from
nineteenth-century Ind

A poster for birth
control in China

WWF ®

World Wide Fund for Nature

Coelacanth, a fossilized fish

Stickers

The four elements—
earth, air, water, fire—and
the signs of the zodiac

A polar bear
in the Arctic

A desert
jerboa

The *Ginkgo biloba* tree
first appeared
265 million
years ago.

A bird
coated in oil
from the wreck
of a tanker

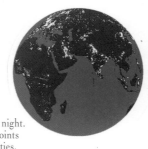

A solar car

The Earth by night.
The white points
represent cities.

Volcanoes

Located within the Pacific Ocean, the Hawaiian chain is comprised of volcanic islands. They come from a hot spot located under the Earth's crust.

An eruption of the Kilauea volcano, Hawaii

A Black Tide

A black tide is a thick, black, sticky layer of oil that has spilled from the hold of an oil tanker damaged on coastal rocks. The oil, lighter than the water, floats on the surface of the sea. It coats birds and seals and smothers plankton, shellfish, and fish. It takes more than ten years for all the species affected by the catastrophe to return to normal.

The *Le Braer,* a ship that sank off the Shetland Islands in the United Kingdom in 1993

The Monsoon

Every year, from March to September, humid winds coming from the Indian Ocean arrive at the coasts of India, bringing torrential downpours to that country. In a single month, 119 to 158 inches (3–4 m) of rain can fall.

In the Country of Ice

Greenland, the "green country," is, in fact, white! It is covered with ice almost the entire year and swept by freezing winds (–58° F, or –50 °C). It nonetheless is home to a population that has learned to protect itself from the cold and to live in desolate places.

The Equatorial Forest

Below the Equator, vegetation is abundant. But people are destroying the forests to get wood or to cultivate new land. By doing so, they are destroying the ecological balance. Meanwhile, the last untouched forests are in danger.

The Sahara Desert

In southern Algeria, the dunes of the Great Western Erg shift continuously because of wind action. Ten thousand years ago, the area received rainfall, but now it's an arid region where there's little life.

Caves

Rainwater soaks into the ground, dissolves the lime- stone, and creates caverns. The limestone collects on the walls and forms stalagmites and stalactites.

Folded Rocks

When continents collide, the rocks undergo tremendous pressure. Compressed, the geological layers fold.

Victoria Falls

The Zambezi River flows in southern Africa between Zimbabwe and Zambia. Vic- toria Falls marks a dramatic break in the river's course. They are 355 feet (108 m) tall and are one of the most famous waterfalls in the world.

When the Earth Quakes

This fissure in a highway was caused by an earthquake and is evidence of continental drift.

The White Cliffs of Étretat, France

In Normandy, on the French coast, 70 million years ago, shells collected at the bottom of the ocean. Twenty million years later, this thick deposit of some several dozen yards (meters) began to rise, making the cliffs of white limestone appear. In Étretat, the peaks and arches stand about a hundred yards (meters) tall. At their base, the waves continue to erode the cliffs, which are slowly becoming hollow.

The Peak of the Young Lady and the town of Étretat, Normandy

Thor's Hammers

Tens of millions of years of flowing water were necessary to shape mountains and dig valleys. Rain and ice also sculpted the surface of the ground and created these forms resembling hammers.

Thor's Hammers, Bryce Canyon National Park, Utah

Titles in the Megascope series

The Adventures of the Great Explorers

Amazing Nature

Infinite Space

Life in the Middle Ages

Mysteries, True and False

Our Planet Earth

The Pharaohs of Ancient Egypt

Searching for Human Origins

Understanding the Human Body

Barron's Educational Series, Inc.
250 Wireless Blvd., Hauppauge, NY 11788